The Art
of
Effective Feedback

ACTIONABLE TIPS AND TECHNIQUES
TO MAKE YOU A BETTER
SUPERVISOR, MANAGER, OR LEADER

Steven Howard

Caliente Press

The Art of Effective Feedback

Actionable Tips and Techniques
to Make You a Better
Supervisor, Manager, or Leader

ISBN: 978-1-943702-74-9 (print edition)
 978-1-943702-78-7 (Kindle edition)

Published by:
Caliente Press
1775 E Palm Canyon Drive, Suite 110-198
Palm Springs, CA 92264
www.CalientePress.com
Email: steven@CalientePress.com

Cover Design: Héctor Castañeda

Contents

Dedication

For Héctor Castañeda

Friend, Artist, Partner.

Always willing to accept feedback.

You make my ideas better
with your creativity and execution.

Thank you for all your wonderful work and support.

Introduction To
The Art of Great Leadership Series

Welcome to *The Art of Great Leadership* series.

Having mentored, coached, and trained over 12,000 people over the past 30 years, I know that transitioning from a highly skilled and excellent Individual Contributor to a supervisor, manager, or team leader position can be quite challenging. There are many reasons for this, some of which will be highlighted below.

But first, the good news. You do not have to let the many transition traps that befall new leaders happen to you. With the right leadership education and coaching, you can be confidently prepared to handle these challenges and obstacles. *The Art of Great Leadership* series aims to put you squarely onto this path.

And, if you desire, you can become a great leader. A leader who is admired. A leader who is trusted. A leader capable of providing the motivation, coaching, feedback, development, and direction that your team members want and need.

Great leadership is an art. It is the art of achieving progress through the involvement and actions of others.

Here are four other things I believe about Great Leadership:

1. Leadership is about both people and results. If you must neglect one, reduce your focus on the

results, for these will come when you have developed your people.

2. Great leaders are great listeners. They know they learn more from listening than from speaking.

3. Great leaders happen at all levels of organizations, not just in the executive suits or the ownership ranks.

4. People development is the single most important long-term priority and responsibility of all leaders at all levels of an organization. Great leaders ensure that this happens.

It is also possible to transition successfully from an Individual Contributor position into a new manager or supervisor role. Unfortunately, this is not a natural or easy transition. Research shows that over 60% of new supervisors and managers fail to transition effectively from individual contributors to new leadership roles.

Transitioning from a successful individual contributor role into a supervisory or manager position is fraught with challenges, concerns, and worries. This is a profound change that requires a new skill set to be successful. It also comes with high risks of failure, personal dissatisfaction, team disenchantment, and team member disengagement.

Why? Simply because too many first-time supervisors and managers are thrown into the deep end of the pool, with little guidance or direction and little or no formal training in leadership skills. They are expected to achieve results through others but often need more people motivation, engagement, feedback, and development skills. They can also have tremendous difficulties communicating unpopular programs and decisions dictated from above and aligning team members with a newly formed strategic vision or change initiatives.

Complicating matters further, numerous pitfalls prevent excellent individual contributors from effectively transitioning into first-time supervisory and managerial responsibilities. Here are 12 transition traps that frequently derail new leaders, managers, and supervisors:

- ✓ Trying to accomplish too much too fast
- ✓ Wearing the "boss" hat too often, too soon
- ✓ Micromanaging due to fear of not knowing everything
- ✓ Trying to mandate buy-in rather than attaining it through influence leadership skills
- ✓ Believing you need to have all the answers
- ✓ Making changes too quickly and too soon
- ✓ Not understanding the priorities of their boss
- ✓ Not knowing their leadership philosophy
- ✓ Not thinking about their leadership mindset
- ✓ Failing to establish boundaries and expectations
- ✓ The inability to prioritize shifting projects, tasks, and deadlines
- ✓ Not knowing how to lead people through change

In *The Art of Great Leadership* book series and the companion *Art of Great Leadership* self-paced, online training program, I will help you overcome and avoid these transition traps.

The Art of Great Leadership collection is a practical, how-to series of informational books to help new and first-time managers and leaders excel in their newfound roles. This series covers the major questions and concerns that supervisors, managers, and leaders have raised with me in conversations over the years.

In each book, I will showcase best practices, tips, and techniques that have turned good managers into great leaders.

Topics we will cover in *The Art of Great Leadership* series include:

- Effective Feedback
- Motivation
- Employee Engagement
- Communicating as a Leader
- Conflict and Drama
- Relationship Building
- Foundations of Leadership
- Workplace Wellbeing
- Creating Cooperative Collaboration
- Transition Traps
- Developing People (and Self)

Please email me at steven@calienteleadership.com with other topics you would like to see included in *The Art of Great Leadership* series.

Here is something else I deeply believe. No leader, manager, or supervisor in today's world should wait around for their boss to tell them how to develop as a leader. It is time for individuals to stop waiting for your company to develop their leadership skills. Likewise, do not waste time on university programs or workshops full of theory but no practicality.

Be proactive. Start leading and controlling your own personal and professional development. To develop your leadership skills, seek leadership education, not a training program.

So, congratulations on being proactive by reading the editions of *The Art of Great Leadership* series that are most applicable to your needs and situation. If I can assist you on your journey, please contact me at steven@calienteleadership.com.

Great Leadership Defined

What is a leader?

In this book, a leader is defined as anyone who directly or indirectly leads people. Full stop.

This includes managers, supervisors, team leaders, first-line leaders, second-line leaders, and those higher in the organization. It also includes entrepreneurs, whether yours is a one-person business or a growing start-up.

I take the definition of a great leader to a higher echelon. I define Great Leadership as *the art of achieving progress through the involvement and actions of others*. Great leaders are strong in both leading people and leading for results, while good leaders typically excel at leading only one or the other.

In truth, everyone is a leader, if only to motivate and lead themselves. Thus, every Individual Contributor should consider themselves a leader as well. And each of you is capable of becoming a great leader.

The mindsets, skills, and behaviors in *The Art of Great Leadership* series will also serve you well in your personal life. Whether you are a parent, involved in community groups, or volunteering as a youth sports coach, applying and exhibiting the leadership skills, tips, and techniques found throughout *The Art of Great Leadership* series will help you in your endeavors.

Introduction

One area of particular weakness in mid-level leaders and new supervisors that I have noticed in my 30 years of international leadership development mentoring, coaching, and training is their inability to provide relevant, useful, beneficial, and effective feedback.

In fact, giving feedback is one of the greatest fears of all new leaders at all levels of organizations.

Why is this? Why do so many supervisors, managers, and leaders fear and shy away from difficult feedback conversations?

The main reason is that no one teaches them how to make these conversations effective. Yet, this is the ONE conversation you, as a people leader, must absolutely never shy away from.

Many leaders, particularly first-time supervisors, team leaders, and managers, are uncomfortable having feedback conversations. When asked why, their replies are typically two-fold:

1) We pay people good money to do good work, so why must I praise them?

2) I fear how they might react if I give them constructive feedback or tell them they are not performing up to expectations.

As I will explain in detail in the first chapter, providing effective feedback requires some mindset changes.

First of all, you want to share feedback, not give feedback. Sharing denotes having a feedback conversation, not a one-way feedback directive and monologue.

Additionally, your purpose or intention of sharing performance feedback is to build competency, capability, and confidence in team members by:

- Reinforcing actions or behaviors that a person is doing well so that they will do so more often or in other circumstances.

- Helping them find ways to change behaviors that are having a negative impact in the workplace or on results.

- Helping them identify and implement ways to improve performance, enhance current skills, and increase self-confidence.

Effective feedback is one of the most important tools you have as a people leader for developing others. Unfortunately, the majority of feedback provided by new (and even experienced) supervisors, team leaders, and managers is ineffective. Such feedback is typified by the feedback provider:

- Telling people what to do instead of engaging them in a respectful conversation.

- Not explaining and discussing the impact and consequences of the person's current performance or behaviors on their results, the team's results, their performance ranking, promotability, relationship with their fellow team members, and their relationship with you as their boss or supervisor.

- Not explaining and discussing the potential benefits of making an enhancing change on the person's current performance or behaviors on their results, the team's results, their performance ranking, promotability, relationship with their fellow team members, and their relationship with you as their boss or supervisor.

- Not explaining and discussing the potential negative consequences of not changing on the person's current performance or behaviors on their results, the team's results, their performance ranking, promotability, relationship with their fellow team members, and their relationship with you as their boss or supervisor.

- Giving feedback that is too vague and general.

- Using universal claims such as "you always" or "you never."

- Delivering feedback that lacks specificity supported by data, evidence, examples, incidences, or observations.

- Not asking the other person for their perspective on what is causing or triggering the situation, results, or behaviors.

- Not asking the other person for their suggestions and ideas on what to change and how to implement a change.

- Not properly prepared in advance.

- Giving feedback only occasionally or on an ad hoc basis.

- Lacking sufficient training in sharing feedback.

- Fearing to be the bearer of bad news.

- Lacking self-confidence in their ability to provide effective feedback.

In summary, most feedback is ineffective because it is one-way and unplanned. It does not motivate change because the feedback provider fails to explain the impact and consequences. The fear of delivering so-called negative feedback decreases self-confidence and results in poor delivery and ineffective discussions.

There is no excuse for giving ineffective feedback. It takes only five – albeit five critical – elements to provide effective feedback:

1) Mindset changes
2) A new language and terminology around feedback
3) An effective feedback model and process
4) Proper preparation
5) Practice, practice, and more practice

There is no need to fear feedback conversations if you incorporate these four elements into your leadership tool kit (as well as the skills we share in the *Communicating as a Leader* edition of *The Art of Great Leadership* series).

Best wishes for continued success,
Steven Howard
September 2024

CHAPTER 1

Mindset Changes

As mentioned previously, providing effective feedback requires some mindset changes.

Let me restate a couple of the key points from the Introduction and then go into more detail and depth.

The first mindset change is that you want to share feedback, not give or deliver feedback to someone. Sharing implies you will have a feedback conversation, not a one-way monologue that dictates what the other person should do.

Most importantly, your mindset regarding your purpose or intention for sharing feedback is to build competency, capability, and confidence in the other person. If your purpose or intention is anything else – such as who's the boss or embarrassing the other person – it is best to walk away and not speak.

You build competency, capability, and confidence in others in three ways:

- Reinforcing actions, thinking, or behaviors that a person is doing well so they will do so more frequently or replicate in other situations.

- Helping them find ways to change behaviors or attitudes that negatively impact results, relationships, collaboration, or performance.

- Helping them identify and implement ways to improve performance, enhance current skills, learn new skills, and increase self-confidence.

There is nothing negative about these three intentions.

Therefore, the best mindset change you can make is to eliminate the terms "positive" and "negative" from your vocabulary describing feedback. If your intention is to help your team member improve their behavior, performance, or confidence, then there is nothing negative about the feedback you will share.

Starting today, alter your terminology and thinking about feedback. Feedback is either fortifying or enhancing – not positive or negative. This is not just a semantic change. Adjusting your mental and verbal verbiage will create a critical transformation in how you think about, prioritize, and plan feedback discussions.

Fortifying Feedback reinforces behaviors and actions while building confidence and competency. Fortifying Feedback is highly motivational and helps the team member know what to repeat or replicate that they are doing well.

Enhancement Feedback aims to improve behaviors and actions while also building confidence and competency.

Enhancement Feedback builds upon the skills, competency, and confidence of the team member, especially if these are low or below expectations.

One key point to note: there is a huge difference between criticism and effective developmental feedback. Criticism, especially when done publicly or in front of others, often destroys confidence and certainly fails to build either competency or capability. However, it builds animosity, disengagement, disloyalty, distrust, and a reluctance to contribute beyond the bare minimum required to remain employed.

To make your feedback more effective, I will give you a proven Effective Feedback Model in the next chapter. In the subsequent chapter, I will also give you best practices and tips on effectively using fortifying and enhancement feedback.

One of the benefits of this mindset change is that you no longer need to be hesitant or procrastinate when there is a need for Enhancement Feedback, as there currently is for "negative" or "constructive" feedback. Since your objective is to help the team member improve, the inclination for hesitancy or procrastination is eradicated.

Naturally, it would be best to incorporate these mindset changes – and the revised feedback terminology – throughout your organization. Hence, I encourage you to use this improved feedback terminology with all those you lead – and with all your peers and colleagues you influence. The more widespread the usage and inculcation of this heightened perspective on feedback, the broader and greater the results you and your organization will attain.

However, you and all of your managerial colleagues can benefit by implementing this new thinking in the areas of the organization you and they lead and influence.

These benefits will include the following:

- More openness and willingness to share and receive feedback.

- Greater trust and respect between you and the people you lead as they see your future feedback as both relevant and beneficially intentional.

- You will enter and engage in feedback discussions with greater confidence.

- You will achieve greater pride in yourself and self-satisfaction, knowing you have done your best to help others grow, improve, and succeed.

Another mindset change is understanding that everyone has the right to decide whether to change their behavior or actions. We cannot change others. We can merely point them in the right direction and encourage them to do so.

However, we also need to point out clearly that they will be held accountable for their decisions to change or not to change. There are, of course, some exclusions where the choice to change is non-negotiable:

- Ethical matters
- Legal matters
- Safety issues

- Compliance policies

- Socially inappropriate behavior or comments

- Processes that absolutely must be followed, especially for safety or product quality reasons.

- Anything with major financial risk implications.

Hence, feedback should come from a place of accountability, empathy, and learning. Accountability in a respectful, helpful, and actionable way.

While this book focuses on workplace feedback – including educational, non-profit, and government organizations – these mindset changes apply equally in your personal and family life. Parents, youth sports coaches, teachers, community leaders, volunteers, and others can achieve greater results through more effective feedback discussions by applying these mindset changes (and the Effective Feedback Model and best practices found in the next two chapters).

A healthy striving for continuous improvement goes to the core intention of effective feedback. Helping people grow while achieving individual and team goals creates team members better positioned and equipped for future success.

With these mindset changes and new terminology, you will be well-positioned to approach feedback discussions with greater confidence.

The next two chapters will provide you with a detailed feedback discussion model and best-practice tips and techniques to help ensure all your future feedback discussions are robust and effective.

CHAPTER 2

Effective Feedback Model

Effective feedback is a process. More accurately, effective feedback is a *continuous* process. It needs to be an ongoing process, not something done on an ad hoc or occasional basis.

One area of particular weakness in mid-level leaders and new supervisors that I have noticed in my 30 years of international leadership development is their inability to give relevant, useful, beneficial, and actionable feedback. This inexperience and a lack of expertise in proper feedback methodology significantly handicaps their ability to lead other team members.

There are nine core components for sharing effective feedback:

- It should be done in a timely manner related to recent output, how a task was handled, or when witnessed behavior needs correcting or modifying. Timeliness regarding a specific incident or before the next likely occurrence is critical.

- It must be provided frequently, not sporadically, or only annually during the formal performance review process.

- It must be delivered and shared with the right intention. Remember, your intention should *always* be to help others build competency, capability, and confidence in their abilities.

- It has to be relevant to the person's tasks and responsibilities.

- It must be specific, not vague.

- It must include sharing the impact of current performance or behavior, as well as the probable impact of making a change and the potential impact of not changing.

- It must be actionable.

- It has to be an interactive process.

- Progress must be monitored and reviewed regularly.

The best methodology for providing effective feedback is to keep Fortifying Feedback and Enhancement Feedback as separate conversations. Rather, have one conversation when you need to share how or what someone is doing well (Fortifying Feedback). Then, have another conversation when you want to share with them an area needing improvement (Enhancement Feedback).

In either case, the purpose of sharing feedback should be to help the other person determine how to change or improve performance (or how to repeat and replicate excellent performance). Every feedback discussion should help the other person (and sometimes yourself) learn and develop.

Use reinforcing feedback (Fortifying Feedback) when you want to reinforce performance or behavior that is producing desired results and outcomes. Your goal here is to recognize what a person is doing well and encourage and motivate them to do so more frequently or in other relevant situations. This improves the likelihood of such performance or behavior being repeated and builds self-confidence in the person receiving such feedback.

Use developmental feedback (Enhancement Feedback) when there is a need to provide corrective instructions or to help someone determine how to change or improve their performance. Again, it is given with the intention of helping that person learn and develop, as well as shaping desired behavior and increasing the likelihood that future performance will be improved.

Additionally, when sharing Enhancement Feedback, do not overload the team member with a litany of areas craving improvement. Instead, focus only on one or two issues to be addressed. Allow them to build some momentum with one or two corrections or changes.

Once you see improvement in these areas, have the next Enhancement Feedback discussion about other issues. However, before you do this, please have at least one Fortifying Feedback conversation acknowledging their efforts to change or improve those initial issues.

It is best not to open and close feedback conversations with toss-aside compliments (the sandwich or bookend approach). Be direct, truthful, and get straight to the point. Be sure to focus on the impact, not the behavior or the performance.

Trying to sugarcoat Enhancement Feedback with pat phrases such as "You are a valued employee, but" only weakens your delivery and no longer works. Everyone knows that "but" or "however" are going to follow opening phrases like "you are doing a good job" or "you did a good job on that task." Everyone knows the hammer is coming down after these perfunctory sentences, so they do neither the employee nor yourself any good. And it makes you appear less than authentic or trustworthy.

For decades, training consultants and firms have advocated the bookend or sandwich approach to feedback. This is the "say something good, then deliver the constructive feedback, and end with a positive comment" approach. Unfortunately, this approach no longer works. As soon as a person hears the opening, *"you are an important member of the team,"* or any other sugarcoating line, the tendency is to tense up immediately and wait for the "but..." segue to some bad news.

The sandwich or bookend approach to feedback makes the recipient feel manipulated. Research published in *Management Review Quarterly* shows that the bookend approach to feedback almost always fails to correct negative or subpar performance. One reason for this is that the recipient focuses more on how the feedback was delivered than on actual performance feedback specifics.

One research study showed that including one sentence when delivering constructive (Enhancement) feedback can increase effectiveness by up to forty percent. That sentence: "*I am giving you these comments because I have very high expectations, and I know that you can reach them.*"

Explaining the importance and impact of the person's actions and behaviors is the most frequently overlooked or omitted step in sharing feedback, which is why most feedback is ineffective.

Without understanding the impact their behaviors or actions are having, there is little internal motivation for the person to make a change. This is why it is extremely important to explain both the impact and importance and to ensure the team member understands these. Part of the explanation of importance and impact is to clearly explain the implications and consequences of not making a change.

Additionally, you will receive less pushback from team members if both the importance of the feedback and the impact are explained. Of course, there is a huge difference between criticism and effective developmental feedback. This may be why the bulk of "constructive feedback" is ineffective since it masquerades as overt criticism.

:

Effective Feedback Discussion Model

Providing effective feedback requires both planning and a process. Here is the feedback discussion model I find to be most effective:

1. Share observations and cite specific incidents, data, examples, or results.

2. Check and verify the other person's perspectives on these observations and facts.

3. State the importance and impact of current actions and behaviors, the probable impact of making a change, and the potential negative consequences if a change is not made.

4. Confirm their understanding of the importance and impact (including the potential impact of not making a change).

5. Seek ideas from the other person for possible solutions and actions to be implemented.

6. Provide alternative ideas for solutions and actions if necessary.

7. Agree on actions to be taken and by when.

8. Confirm the progress monitoring process and timing.

9. Thank them and express gratitude and confidence.

The main benefit of this feedback discussion model is that both parties will see this as a discussion, not a one-way conversation. Most importantly, the team member will understand the importance and impact of their behaviors and actions and the potential consequences if a change is not made.

Additionally, the team member "owns" the solution if theirs is the chosen action agreed upon. After all, it was their idea, not something you dictated or generated. When having this conversation, be sure to elicit the possible solutions from the team member first, even if you already have a solid notion of the solution. Yes, this takes a little more time. However, the occurrence of buy-in and implementation improve markedly.

It is best that the solution idea comes from them without your prompting or suggestion. People are more likely to implement changes if they know the importance and impact of their actions, understand the impact of making/not making the change, and have input into what and how the change will be made.

Sometimes, you will face a situation where the team member cannot think of a possible solution or action in the moment. That is fine. Great leaders know that feedback is a process and that not everything can be resolved in a single conversation. If the issue is not urgent, give the team member a couple of days to think of possible solutions and arrange to meet again within 48 to 72 hours.

This builds trust and confidence as it shows you are willing to give them time to think through what you have said about the importance and impact of their actions and behavior. And, it provides time for them to come up with potential solutions.

It also shows your willingness to listen to their ideas rather than imposing your own remedies.

The other critical part of this process is to discuss how and when progress monitoring will occur. By agreeing to regular reviews based on time periods or specific milestones, expectations for monitoring and oversight are settled. Thus, the employee will not feel micromanaged and the leader will not feel like they have abandoned a struggling team member.

Remember, you want to share feedback, not give feedback. Also, not sharing feedback means an employee will continue performing below expectations. So, if you do not share feedback on their performance and agree on corrective actions and progress monitoring, and their performance does not improve, the onus is on you. Not sharing Enhancement Feedback is truly callous and certainly less kind than having the feedback conversation (especially if the feedback conversation has the intention of helping the team member improve performance or behavior and is a true, interactive discussion).

Crushing people during difficult feedback conversations is evidence of the lack of communication skills in the leader. Not using an appropriate model and format for having hard conversations around performance and behavior results in these conversations going astray and being ineffective. The model above is a proven, best-practice method for ensuring these hard conversations provide effective feedback that produces results.

Great Leaders combine kindness and respect with empathy and valuable straight talk, resulting in effective feedback conversations. After all, innovation, creativity, passion, and engagement are incompatible with and rarely found when feedback is formulated around shame and blame.

I recommend that the timing of progress monitoring should be based either on regular calendar updates (such as every other Tuesday afternoon) or on reaching certain milestones (such as the completion of initial data analysis). This way, both parties know exactly when progress update discussions will occur.

Typically, progress monitoring happens ad hoc, often when the manager or leader suddenly finds a few minutes of open time on their calendar. In such instances, the leader proactively reaches out to the team member and asks *"How's it going?"* type questions. The problem with this approach is that it catches the team member unprepared and ill-equipped for the discussion. Also, this often feels like a micromanaging approach from the team member's perspective.

However, when progress monitoring discussions happen according to an agreed-upon timetable, the team member is more likely to consider these talks to be microcoaching sessions rather than micromanaging.

The benefits of this feedback discussion model are plentiful:

- Both parties will see this as a discussion, not a one-way conversation.

- The team member receiving the feedback understands the importance and impact of their actions and behaviors – and the potential consequences if a change is not made.

- The team member "owns" the solution if theirs is the chosen action agreed upon.

- The team member understands how and when progress monitoring will take place.

- The ongoing feedback and progress monitoring discussions eliminate surprises during the annual performance review.

Effective Feedback

Feedback is also a factor in increasing employee engagement, but only if it is done properly. A leader's intention in giving feedback to a team member must always be to help the employee improve performance or behavior. Feedback should never be given when upset, angered, or disappointed with a direct report or colleague.

Additionally, the purpose of feedback should never be to belittle or disparage an employee, make anyone feel less-than-adequate, or punish a team member. And, of course, scolding an employee is neither a form of coaching nor proper engagement-inducing feedback.

This is not to say there is no place for corrective feedback in the workplace. Part of personal development means learning from mistakes and errors. If someone is doing something wrong, then corrective feedback is mandatory. However, it will only be engagement-inducing and productive feedback if such corrective feedback is given *with the intention of helping* the other person improve performance or behavior. Thus, leaders must offer feedback that helps and inspires team members to perform at higher, more productive levels, not cut them down to size through criticism, ridicule, or denigrating remarks.

All feedback should be delivered in an ongoing, timely, and non-judgmental manner. It must also be specific, descriptive, detailed, actionable, and future-focused. You are not looking for ownership of blame here or excuses. You are looking for ways to improve future performance or to correct unacceptable behavior.

Ineffective feedback is a focus on the past. Effective feedback has a focus on the future. Here are the differences:

Ineffective Feedback	Effective Feedback
Emphasis on the past	Emphasis on the future
Describes what happened	Suggestions and agreement on what to do next
Focused on what did and did not go well	Focuses on how the person can develop and progress
The person giving the feedback does most of the talking	The person receiving the feedback does most of the talking
Highlight errors	Asks, "What would you do differently next time?"
Can be very time-consuming	Leverages time effectively

Can lead to people feeling judged	Emphasis is on the person's development without judgment, blame, or shame
People receiving feedback can take comments personally and get defensive.	People receiving the feedback comments are motivated as it focuses on improvement

Leaders in my classroom and coaching sessions often complain that people are not motivated to change. That those working for them are too set in their ways. The truth is far more likely that these leaders have not figured out how to motivate their direct reports. And that previous feedback sessions did not include the importance and impact elements.

After reluctant admission to these truths, these leaders and managers understand why their feedback efforts have often been ineffective. My next step is to mentor them on why healthy striving for improvement and excellence are intrinsic motivators for almost everyone.

Great leaders know how to leverage these stimuli. Intrinsic motivators are far superior in stimulating change than extrinsic motivators, such as money, recognition, and punishment.

Great leaders make ongoing feedback an expectation. They also encourage and normalize requests for feedback from team members. When all feedback is designed to reinforce or enhance performance and confidence, the results-producing elements of productivity, innovation, and cooperative collaboration are bound to increase.

Clear Line of Value

One additional factor people want and need to succeed is knowing how they provide value. People are more fulfilled when given a chance to contribute to a team's or an organization's success. Too often, however, leaders do not tell employees how their efforts provide value to a team objective, a department goal, or an organizational strategy. It is what I call a Clear Line of Value.

In recent months, a lot has been written about the need for organizations to emphasize corporate purpose and mission to connect with current and future workforces. And there is a lot to be said for this. Since the pandemic, people have been re-evaluating their purposes and priorities in life and the role that work plays in these.

While this is a great place to start to define and communicate the purposeful intention of the organization, mission, and vision statements quickly start to wear thin. Especially when people do not understand their role or contribution in helping the organization or the team drive toward obtaining such objectives and goals.

The way to entice cooperative collaboration is by ensuring every individual contributor on your team knows and understands the value contributions they are making. This goes a lot deeper than being told they are "an important team member" or a "valued contributor."

Rather, leaders need to explain – and constantly reinforce – the specifics of how each team member adds value to a project, the team, a departmental goal, or an organizational strategy.

All employees should understand the Clear Line of Value they are providing. Otherwise, tasks become busy work. Jobs are viewed as personally unsatisfying. Personal motivation wanes. Collaboration decreases as little value is perceived in cooperating.

Knowing that the work one is doing provides value is intrinsically motivating. Intrinsic motivation is much more powerful than extrinsic motivation. When you explain to people how their efforts provide value to other parts of the organization or customers, they become more fulfilled, energized, motivated, and engaged.

Not only should you regularly highlight this Clear Line of Value to your team members, but you should also have discussions about value contributions. Ask them, "Where did you contribute a lot of value last week?" or "What value did you contribute to that project?"

Are their responses in line with your observations? If so, reconfirm that their contributions were important and why. If not, add your thoughts and perspectives on their Clear Line of Value.

If people know their work is important and adds value, their engagement and productivity levels increase. Absent this knowledge, their jobs become dull, routine, and boring. And they tune out and disengage.

Impact of Feedback on Motivation

There are two types of motivations that propel us into action: intrinsic and extrinsic motivation.

Extrinsic motivation comes from external factors or outside rewards. It happens when we are driven to perform a task or engage in an activity to earn a reward from others or to avoid punishment or something negative happening to us. Opposite to this is intrinsic motivation, which is the drive to engage in activities for their inherent satisfaction and the personal rewards we give ourselves. When intrinsically motivated, we do things because we find them inherently interesting, enjoyable, or satisfying, not because of an external reward or pressure.

As you can see, intrinsic motivation comes from within. Personal interest, desires, enjoyment, or a sense of self-satisfaction or self-fulfillment drive it. This internal drive has nothing to do with positive extrinsic motivators such as money, power, position, recognition, or praise. Nor does it have anything to do with a desire to avoid negative outcomes such as punishment, criticism, or being excluded from groups or activities.

Without a doubt, intrinsic motivating factors are more powerful as they lead to:

> Sustained engagement – actions and activities
> driven by intrinsic motivation are more likely to be

:

sustained over time because they are inherently satisfying.

Higher quality of work, innovation, and involvement – intrinsically motivated people often put more effort into their work and other activities, leading to better quality, creativity, and innovation. They also tend to be more mentally and emotionally engaged in their activities.

Personal growth and wellbeing – intrinsic motivation is closely linked to personal fulfillment, generating greater wellbeing, self-esteem, and personal growth.

Autonomy and ownership – intrinsic motivation often involves a sense of autonomy and ownership over one's actions, thus fostering a deeper connection to the task or activity.

Here are ten of the most commonly found intrinsic motivators in people:

Autonomy – the desire to have control over one's actions and decisions.

Mastery – the drive to improve and master a skill or knowledge area.

Purpose – the motivation to do something meaningful and contribute to a larger purpose or cause bigger than oneself.

Curiosity – the innate desire to learn and explore more things.

Passion – the drive to engage in activities one loves or feels strongly about.

Challenge – the enjoyment that results from overcoming difficult tasks or solving problems.

Creativity – the desire to express oneself creatively, develop new ideas, or innovate.

Personal Growth – the motivation for continuous growth and development as an individual, both professionally and personally.

Recognition – the internal satisfaction resulting from self-recognition and self-appreciation for one's efforts. This is not related to external praise, rewards, or awards.

Connection – the desire to build and maintain meaningful relations.

Importance of Recognition

It is also important for leaders to acknowledge progress, small successes, and incremental wins. Change happens best when leaders recognize effort and reward results.

Remember, team members want reinforcing feedback. They want to know how and when they are producing good work. Hence, the motivational aspect of Fortifying Feedback is extremely high.

Unfortunately, many leaders do not do this for fear that people will become complacent and slow down. Instead, they push, push, push. Not surprisingly, burnout increases significantly. Results are not achieved. Employee attrition increases. Those remaining become more stressed. And workplace harmony is nowhere in sight.

Great leaders practice gratitude. They know that openly celebrating successes and wins leads team members to

:

increase their individual and collective efforts. Recognition of effort is highly motivational. Recognizing progress replenishes people, refuels their energy levels, and reignites their passions. That is much better than having a team of burnt-out souls struggling to get through the workday.

The rule of recognition is simple: Your default setting is to focus on what a person does right and make a point to commend the person for those positive actions, sincerely and specifically. The three key benefits of this are:

- Encourages the person to continue those positive behaviors

- Builds trust and psychological safety

- Makes it easier to share Enhancement Feedback in the future

There is a difference between being tough-minded when it comes to decision-making and being tough-minded when dealing with team members. Replace the desire to show "tough love" to an employee with a willingness to express compassion and enhancement feedback to a human being who happens to be on your team.

This does not mean that straight-talk conversations should not be held, particularly with someone whose performance is not up to expectations. The difference is in the manner in which the conversation is held. This includes the tonality you use and how balanced you are in expressing your viewpoints and soliciting inputs and possible corrective actions from the team member.

You can be compassionate and still hold people accountable. You can display empathy and still point out ways a person can improve their performance or their behavior. You can be gentle and kindhearted while helping someone understand the negative impact their performance or behavior is having. As long as you do so authentically.

Impact of Feedback on Trust
Trust is foundational to leadership. If a leader is not trusted by the people they lead – and their colleagues and peers – nothing else they do matters. You cannot be an optimal leader if you are not trusted.

Unfortunately, there is not a great deal of trust in the workplace place today. Surveys consistently show that over half of employees do not trust their employer.

For example, a study by Davis Associates revealed that 57% of employees have little or no trust in their leaders. A similar survey from EY showed that less than half of employees (46%) placed "a great deal of trust" in their employers, while 15% indicated they had very little or no trust at all in their employers. The remaining 39% said they have "some trust" in their employers, which is not exactly a ringing endorsement of their leadership.

Unfortunately, the lack of trust in the workplace is a two-way street. The lack of trust in employees by managers reduces inclusion, productivity, innovation, and results. A 2021 study

41

:

by the Workforce Institute found that a lack of trust by bosses directly impacts how employees have a sense of belonging (64%), their career choices (58%), and their mental health (55%). Additionally, 24% of the survey respondents said they had left a company because they did not feel trusted. I suspect this figure is higher for the millions who are part of the Great Resignation.

That same survey shared how employees believe managers can earn higher levels of trust: being dependable (52%), being honest (34%), actively listening (28%), providing helpful feedback (25%), and caring about employee wellbeing (22%).

The top five factors influencing the lack of trust in bosses globally were:

1. Is not open or transparent in communication
2. Is not appreciative / does not provide recognition or praise for a job well done
3. Does not communicate with me enough
4. Does not value my point of view
5. Does not make wise business decisions

As you can see, poor communication and ineffective feedback are at the heart of mistrust.

Asking questions and actively listening to others are trust-building behaviors. People are more willing to trust you when you ask for their input and know you will listen to their ideas, suggestions, issues, and concerns.

When feedback is combined with forgiveness, leaders are more likely to prompt and motivate changes that result in better performance and improved behavior.

The next chapter includes specific actions and best practices for using the Effective Feedback Model.

:

CHAPTER 3

Best Practices For Using The Effective Feedback Model

Having a proven model for providing effective feedback is great. Knowing how to use the model is even better! That is the focus of this chapter.

First, I will share best-practice tips for using the Effective Feedback Discussion Model during Fortifying Feedback discussions. Then, I will do the same for Enhancement Feedback discussions.

To save you from going back and forth between chapters, here is the Effective Feedback Discussion Model:

1. Share observations

2. State the importance and impact of actions and behaviors

3. Check and verify the perspectives of the other person on observations

4. Confirm understanding of the importance and impact

5. Seek ideas from the other person for possible solutions and actions to be taken

6. Provide alternative ideas for solutions and actions if necessary

7. Agree on actions to be taken and by when

8. Confirm the progress monitoring process and timing

9. Thank them and express gratitude and confidence

Effective feedback requires time, commitment, and courage. Fortunately, the reward is the continuous growth of your people and the creation of a thriving development and performance culture for your team and organization.

However, development and change only occur when feedback is specific and actionable.

Fortifying Feedback Discussions

In Fortifying Feedback discussions, only the first four steps of the Effective Feedback Discussion model are usually needed.

Remember, Fortifying Feedback discussions are designed to reinforce behaviors and actions that the team member is doing well and to build their competency, capabilities, and confidence in these areas.

Too often, the only reinforcing feedback team members ever hear is a hearty *"good job"* or *"thanks for doing X."* Or, at the most, *"You did a great job on that presentation this morning."*

While there is nothing wrong with hearing such compliments from one's supervisor or manager, there is no tangibility or specificity. But such phrases are not actionable.

Hence, while the team member may feel warm and fuzzy upon receiving such compliments, such statements have little or no value. The person has no idea exactly what they did well, nor do they have a clue on what aspects of their work they should repeat or replicate in the future. They also will not understand the importance or impact of what they did well.

Let me take that last example (telling someone they did a great job on the presentation) and show how to add both specificity and tangibility to the praise:

> *Hi Susan. I thought you did a really good job in the presentation this morning.*
>
> *I particularly thought you were well prepared and did a good job emphasizing the key points.*
>
> *Also, you did an excellent job answering the questions raised during the presentation. In fact, I think the way you carefully listened to and clarified the questions before responding helped build credibility both in you and in the material you presented.*
>
> *Again, well done. Thanks for doing such a great job.*

This more detailed example of reinforcing feedback is much more powerful and effective than the nonspecific "you did a great job on the presentation" comment. Now, team member Susan knows exactly what she should continue doing in future presentations (preparation, emphasizing key points, and carefully listening and clarifying questions from the audience).

Additionally, these four paragraphs will undoubtedly go a long way in building her self-confidence in her presentation skills and ability to field questions.

Also, notice how this feedback is specific regarding sharing observations and incorporates both the importance and impact elements. In this case, the key impact was building credibility in both the presenter (Susan) and the content of her presentation. The important elements were her preparation and emphasizing the key points. This feedback also underscores the importance of carefully listening to and clarifying the questions raised so that Susan responds, rather than reacts, to them.

Best of all, these four paragraphs take less than 40 seconds to deliver. Hence, not having time to deliver effective Fortifying Feedback is not a valid excuse. This is one of the advantages of separating the Fortifying Feedback and Enhancement Feedback discussions. You can share frequent and regular Fortifying Feedback conversations without carving out large time slots on your calendar.

With only the first four steps of the Effective Feedback Discussion Model being used, Fortifying Feedback is often a one-way conversation or message. There is no need to ask the team member, "*What do you think went well?*" or "*What are your takeaways from completing this assignment?*" Those questions are best reserved for status review and project completion meetings.

A Fortifying Feedback discussion is best conducted in a face-to-face meeting. Of course, that is not always possible in our world of remote and hybrid workers. When the discussion cannot be held in person, it is acceptable to hold it via a phone or virtual call. You can even deliver the message by email, text, or instant message – provided you follow it up soon after with a call or face-to-face meeting.

A word of caution: be careful when praising someone in front of others. Not everyone likes or enjoys public praise. And in some cultures, it is flat wrong to do so. One way to gauge if a person is uncomfortable with public recognition is how they respond to such acclaim. If they automatically and instinctively respond with "*it wasn't me, it was a team effort*" or similar phrases, that often indicates that public recognition is not for them.

The same is true if they become overtly shy and step away when they are being publicly lauded. When you see this, provide future praise and recognition privately.

Enhancement Feedback Discussions

Unlike Fortifying Feedback, Enhancement Feedback discussions should almost always take place in a face-to-face and confidential manner. The only exception is when distance is a barrier, in which case a video call (to observe body language) or a phone call can be substituted.

If the feedback discussion cannot occur face-to-face, that is not a reason to postpone it for more than a few days. Timeliness is a critical component of Enhancement Feedback, especially for important issues that are better corrected or amended now rather than later. An exception to this is anything that is not mission-critical, such as presentation or writing skills.

The entire Effective Feedback Discuss Model must be covered for Enhancement Feedback, which may require more than one conversation. These multiple conversations are not a replacement for your ongoing feedback conversations. They simply indicate that the situation warrants several conversations to cover all nine Effective Feedback Discussion Model steps.

Let me walk you through an effective feedback discussion using the same scenario as above of Susan's presentation.

Imagine we are now three weeks later. I walk by her office and see she is working on an updated status report presentation to the working group.

Knock. Knock.

Me: Hi Susan. I see you are working on the presentation for next week's meeting. How is it going?

Susan: Fine. Good, actually. I am just pulling together the updated figures.

Me: Great. Do you have a moment? I want to discuss something about the last presentation with you.

Susan: Sure. What is that?

Me: I have been thinking about that presentation, which, as you will recall, went very well. But there was one area where I thought you could improve.

Susan: Okay, go on.

Me: Do you recall those three slides in the middle that had a great deal of text on them?

Susan: Yes. Those were difficult to get through.

Me: Yes. And I noticed that when those slides were on the screen, the audience was reading the slides and no longer listening to you. Did you notice that as well?

Susan: No, not really. I think I was too focused on getting through all that data.

Me: That is understandable. But you want to keep their attention on you and what you are saying, right?

Susan: Yes, of course.

Me: What could you do differently in next week's presentation?

Susan: I am not sure. Maybe have fewer words on the slides. Or use some pictures to illustrate the context of the key data points.

Me: Would you feel comfortable doing either of those things?

Susan: Sure. Let me think about which way makes the most sense.

Me: Sounds good. I look forward to seeing which direction you decide to take. And we should both monitor the audience next week to see if they spend more time listening to you than reading the slides.

Susan: Okay. Thank you.

Me: No. Thank you.

Notice how easily each step of the Effective Feedback Conversation Model is incorporated into this short talk:

1. Specific observations are stated on the three slides with heavy text.

2. Checking with Susan to verify if she had the same observations or perspectives.

3. The impact of how too much text stopped the audience from listening to her and focusing instead on reading the slides. The importance of her wanting the audience to stay focused on her and her words.

4. Ensuring confirmation that Susan understands the importance of keeping the audience focused on her.

5. Seeking ideas from Susan for possible solutions.

6. Provide alternative ideas (if necessary, which was not in this scenario).

7. Agree on the actions to be taken.

8. Confirming that we will both monitor during next week's presentation.

9. Thanking her. (Gratitude and confidence would mostly be conveyed through nonverbal body language and tone of voice.)

Note also how I get directly into the Enhancement Feedback discussion without using the sandwich or bookend approach.

There is no need for generalized statements of what a solid performer Susan is or what a wonderful presenter she is. One quick reference to the last presentation, which went well, helps both parties concentrate on the specifics of that presentation only.

Also, note that regarding timeliness, I have elected to have the Enhancement Feedback discussion with Susan as she prepares her next presentation. Since this is a presentation she gives regularly, there is no need to give such Enhancing Feedback right after the last presentation. This allows the motivational and positive aspects of the Fortifying Feedback given immediately after the previous presentation to sink in and build her self-confidence.

Now, admittedly, this Enhancement Feedback conversation takes more time than if I walked into Susan's office and said:

Hi Susan. In your presentation three weeks ago, you had three slides containing too much text. That is not good. Please divide those slides into multiple slides, each with less text. Thanks.

In the first of these two scenarios, Susan offers an acceptable solution to me as her manager. Since it is her idea, she will have higher buy-in and willingness to implement this solution.

In the second scenario, the solution is mine and mandated by me. While Susan may reluctantly implement this solution, she may not be happy about it and likely will not be highly

:

committed to it. She may even be irritated and incensed by being told how to "fix" her presentation.

The second scenario is how a manager would handle the situation – by giving directions and dictating the solution. The first scenario is how a great leader would handle the situation – by engaging with the other person, seeking their ideas and inputs, and encouraging their ideas and suggested solutions.

Sure, the exact same results are achieved. But think about the negative impact on my relationship with Susan in the second example. Will she see me trusting her? Will she think I value her ideas and suggestions? Definitely not. Will she want to continue working for me? Doubtful. At least not when another job opportunity comes her way.

What if the Team Member Disagrees?

Of course, not all Enhancement Feedback conversations will go as smoothly as above.

What if the team member disagrees or does not want to make a change? How should you handle that?

Here is what I would do if Susan disagreed that a change needs to be made. The first part of the conversation remains the same, up until the point where she disagrees.

Knock. Knock.

Me: Hi Susan. I see you are working on the presentation for next week's meeting. How is it going?

Susan: Fine. Good, actually. I am just pulling together the updated figures.

Me: Great. Do you have a moment? I want to discuss something about the last presentation with you.

Susan: Um. What is that?

Me: I have been thinking about that presentation, which, as you will recall, went very well. But there was one area where I thought you could improve.

Susan: Yes, it went very well. I am not sure it needs any improvement.

Me: Do you recall those three slides in the middle that had a great deal of text on them?

Susan: Yes. Those were difficult to get through. But the information in them is very important.

Me: Yes, the information is extremely important. But I noticed that when those slides were on the screen, the audience was reading the slides and no longer listening to you. Do you notice that as well?

Susan: No, not really.

Me: That is understandable. But you want to keep their attention on you and what you are saying, right?

Susan: Yes, of course.

Me: What could you do differently in next week's presentation?

Susan: Preferably nothing. I do not want to make any changes. I like the format and flow of the presentation. And people are used to it. Plus, I have a dozen things on my plate and do not have time to rewrite the presentation.

Me: I understand. And I certainly do not think the entire presentation needs to be rewritten. But perhaps a few amendments to those three slides might be in order.

Susan: I would rather not. If people read those slides, so be it. And if I think they have not heard what I have said, I will repeat myself.

Me: Okay, that is one way to handle it. Another might be to divide those three slides into multiple slides, with less text on each one.

Susan: I really do not want to do that. There are already so many sides in the slide deck. And I do not want to go over my allotted time. The project manager hates it when people do that.

Me: Okay, keep the slides as they are. But let us both monitor the audience while those three slides are on screen and evaluate if their attention has moved to the slides and away from you. We do want to keep them focused on you and your words.

Susan: Okay. Thank you.

Me: No. Thank you.

Sometimes, as a leader, you must allow team members to learn from their mistakes. In this scenario, I would be confident that allowing Susan to continue the next presentation with a few text-heavy slides will raise her awareness of losing the attention of her audience.

I would also handle this conversation differently if I thought the team member was being set up for failure. But this is a regular presentation to a working group and thus is not mission-critical. On the other hand, if the next presentation were to a senior executive in the organization and a poor presentation would reflect badly on her, I would have a different and more persuasive (maybe even directive) conversation with her.

As you can see, how you handle Enhancement Feedback conversations will vary depending on the nature of the topic, your ability to engage the other person in a dialogue, the flow of the discussion, and their willingness to make a change. This is another reason I believe leadership is an art. You must remain agile and adaptable to be a great leader.

Best Practice Tips for Enhancement Feedback Conversations

Enhancement feedback discussions should never be held when either party is angry or emotionally upset, unless in an emergency or when absolutely necessary (to ascertain the situation status or determine the root cause of something that has gone wrong). When either party is distraught or agitated, the feedback discussion should be postponed (or adjourned if already underway) and continued two to three days later. The same applies if your team member gets overly emotional or stressed during the conversation.

Always minimize or eliminate physical impediments to collaboration, such as sitting across a large conference room table or holding the discussion in your office (your place of

:

power). You want to create an environment of equilibrium and harmony.

The main negative ingredient to effective feedback comes when managers want to give feedback (one-way monologues) rather than share feedback (having actual discussions that engage the other person).

Without a doubt, all Enhancement Feedback discussions must be planned and practiced. This point cannot be overemphasized. The lack of planning may be the number one reason for Enhancement Feedback discussions going astray. I will provide you with some best-practice tips regarding planning in the next chapter.

One last point about Enhancement Feedback conversations. Be sure to document all discussions, as your Human Resources department will request this if a team member's performance issue deteriorates into a formal Performance Improvement Plan (PIP) situation. The best way to document the discussion is with a follow-up email specifying areas and topics that were discussed, the actions to be taken by the team member, the actions you will take, and confirmation of the progress monitoring process and timing of such.

Suppose the team member's performance continues to decline or fails to meet expectations or standards. In that case, HR will ask you for documentation of your efforts to help the person improve. If you have such documentation, HR will be your friend and help you take the situation to the next level. Without such documentation, you will be at square one and have to begin a lengthy, and often troublesome, process from scratch.

:

CHAPTER 4

Keys For Success

Like all communication conducted by leaders of people, integral to effective feedback success is preparation and practice. Unfortunately, too much communication by leaders is done ad hoc, with little or no preparation or practice. This is a mistake. And one that almost always results in ineffective or less-than-optimal feedback discussions.

However, planning the conversation is only part of your task. There is one more critical preparation element for success in sharing effective feedback: your mental presence. Your active engagement and responsibility for how you will enter the conversation and maintain composure throughout are crucial.

Planning Your Words

Planning what you will say and ask is more crucial for Enhancement Feedback than for Fortifying Feedback. However, it's always beneficial to plan your word choice, specific examples, and questions for both types of feedback. Equally important is planning your body language, voice tonality, and posture to ensure they support your verbal feedback.

This planning incorporates more than you might expect and includes:

- What you want to say
- What questions you want to ask
- The follow-up questions you want to employ
- The suggestions you have for making improvements
- How will you wrap up and summarize the discussion (including highlighting the next steps and monitoring milestones)
- The environment in which the discussion will be held
- Your mindset going into the discussion

The first point is obvious. You must collect all your recorded observations, data, examples, and results to share in step one of the Feedback Discussion Model presented in an earlier chapter. Additionally, you need to plan how to clearly and concisely link this information to why they are important and the impact being created. This focused and effective communication is one of the most important keys to effective feedback.

When you think about the links to impact, you should consider expressing the impact on individual output, the department's or team's results, and the perception of the department or team by other departments or customers. You should also contemplate sharing how the team member's performance or behavior impacts their relationships with other team members, colleagues, and even yourself as their supervisor or manager.

Planning your questions is also important, as having these pre-planned will give you greater confidence going into the conversation. Also, planned questions are almost always better than ones created off the top of your head in mid-conversation.

A best practice is to ask questions about the causes of situations even when you already know the answer. While this may seem like a waste of time, it is best to let team members describe the origins or reasons for a situation in their own words. Doing so goes a long way in helping the team member take ownership or responsibility for their decisions, actions, and behaviors. Again, you are not seeking to blame or shame the other person, just enabling them to see and understand their role in the situation under discussion.

Plus, with this approach, you may learn something you were unaware of. Additionally, plan your follow-up questions, especially for those where you can accurately predict the response. Some great follow-up questions are:

> *Please tell me more about that.*
>
> *Why do you think that happened?*
>
> *Is this the outcome you expected? Why or why not?*

:

Digging deeper, tell me more about the background that led to this decision.

Is there anything else you can add? Any more details?

Note the open-ended nature of these questions. Your aim is to gain an insight into their thinking and decision-making processes. So, refrain from asking closed-ended questions that only elicit one-word or short responses.

As mentioned previously, you want to solicit ideas and potential solutions for any course corrections from the other person. Again, your questions should be planned and practiced so they are delivered in a natural, friendly, and non-threatening manner.

What do you do if the other person says they cannot think of any ideas or does not know what solutions to suggest? This can be highly frustrating unless you are prepared for it. The best way to prepare for this is to have a standard phrase you have practiced and can deliver with authenticity and genuineness. Here is mine (when they say something like they have no idea what to do):

That is okay. This is an important topic for both of us. How about we both take a couple of days to think about possible solutions and ideas? And then, let's share some options and possibilities. I really want to hear your thoughts and ideas. How does (Thursday at 10:30) work for you?

This approach is a strong trust builder, showing the team member that you truly and authentically want to hear their thoughts and ideas. Plus, it demonstrates your willingness to give them time to think. After all, asking them for potential solutions or ways to change on the spot may have caught them off guard. They may be unable to think of something in the moment, so giving them 48-72 hours to contemplate puts them at greater ease.

One mistake that many new managers and leaders make is they interpret the inability of others to offer solutions and ideas in the moment as an opening for them to insert their own ideas. As the previous chapter showed, putting forth our ideas and solutions may lead to reluctant action and minimal or no buy-in. Remember, you are playing the long game here. Not everything needs to be resolved or agreed upon in a single discussion. Let the team member have time to think. After all, you have been thinking about this discussion in advance. Now it is time to allow them to do the same.

Importantly, you must also plan *what you **do not** want to say*. This may seem strange, but often, people get into feedback discussions and say something off the top of their heads that sends the conversation in the wrong direction. One of the most frequent examples of this is the phrase *this is not meant to be a criticism*. Well, congratulations. Using this phrase has put the proverbial elephant in the room. Everything the manager says after this phrase has been uttered will undoubtedly be taken as criticism by the other person.

:

Other phrases to avoid:

This is not a big deal, but... (Why are you discussing it if it is not a big deal?)

Don't take this the wrong way... (How else do you expect them to take it?)

Please do not overreact to this... (Puts the other person on the defensive and moves them into an emotional, non-rational state.)

I can see that you are upset. (Will be immediately and instinctively denied, which turns the discussion into an argument about their emotional state.)

Planning the Conversation

Conversations are dynamic. While it is best to plan them, we must remain flexible and adaptable as they tend to go in all sorts of directions.

To minimize this happening, plan how to start and end the discussion:

- How will you build rapport at the start (and throughout the conversation)?

- How will you segue into the feedback conversation?

- How will you wrap up and summarize the next steps?

These three elements will help you determine the flow of the conversation that you will lead. And yes, there is a need to balance the conversation so neither person dominates the discussion. However, your responsibility as the supervisor or manager is to lead the talk. You must maintain control of the conversation, particularly its flow, and ensure all key points and questions are raised, answered, and discussed.

You also have to ensure the conversation stays within the expected time allocation. It is easier to maintain control of the conversation when you establish some personal rapport initially rather than jumping directly into the feedback discussion.

You can (and should) build rapport throughout the conversation. However, this is especially critical at the start of the discussion. This creates a connection between you and the team member and helps to ease into the feedback discussion. All it takes is one or two quick questions as a bridge into the talk:

> *How are you doing?*
>
> *How is the family?*
>
> *The last time we spoke, you mentioned (something). How is that going?*

The important thing here is to keep the initial rapport-building short, sweet, and authentic. Do not ask questions about something that you are truly not interested in. They will see through the façade and any inauthenticity, putting you immediately on the back foot and destroying trust.

Building rapport at the beginning of a feedback conversation is a much-improved method over the throw-away lines used in the sandwich and bookend approaches to

:

feedback, such as *"you are doing great work, but..."* and *"we really value your contributions, but..."* Those disposable lines are wasteful and do nothing to put the team member at ease or ready to engage in the conversation.

Active listening is one of the best ways to build rapport and trust. You start active listening by being fully present in the conversation, turning off potential distractions like mobile phones and instant messaging systems, and turning off your brain on all other topics or projects on your plate. Eye contact, body posture, paraphrasing what the other says, and asking follow-up questions are among the best ways to display you are actively listening.

These methods work equally as well for virtual conversations held over video links as in face-to-face conversations. Another way to show that you are actively listening in the virtual environment is to lean into your camera when the other person is talking. This shows that you are focused on them and their words. You can enhance this through nonverbal cues, such as nodding your head, giving a thumbs-up or other hand gestures, smiling, and other facial expressions.

A great way to build rapport for future conversations is by expressing gratitude and thanking them for sharing their thoughts, ideas, and comments. You should also thank them for being engaged in the conversation. This sets up future conversations for success. Remember, feedback is an ongoing process of frequent conversations.

Segueing into the feedback conversation from a few moments of rapport building is an art, one in which you will get better through practice and experience. My preferred way to segue into the conversation is by being direct and straightforward:

> *I would like to discuss an important area of professional development with you and exchange thoughts and ideas on possible changes we could implement. I think this will take us approximately (xx) minutes. Is this a good time for you to have a conversation on this?*
>
> (Then, assuming they say "yes.")
>
> *Great. But first, is there any other topic or situation you want to discuss if we have time?*

This approach accomplishes four things:

a) you share the general nature of the conversation,

b) you check to ensure that the other person is mentally and emotionally prepared for the conversation,

c) you check that the other person is not time-constrained and can engage in a productive conversation, and

d) you find out what else is on their mind.

As for the last point, you can lead the conversation as planned or tackle their topic if you deem it more important.

69

:

You also do not have to commit to discussing their subject, especially if you reply, *"Great. If we have time to discuss that now, we will. If not, we will schedule time for a separate conversation."*

This conveys that the professional development conversation is more important and that you want to ensure appropriate time is given to it. This reply also shows that you have listened to and acknowledged their topic and will devote time to discuss it with them later.

Note that I do not mention the word feedback in the above segue. Unfortunately, this word resonates with negative connotations and has an adverse stigma attached to it. Also, note the use of "we language" in my segue:

> *discuss with you* (shows this will be a dialogue, not a monologue)
>
> *exchange some thoughts and ideas* (invites the other person to share openly and establishes the expectation that they will participate in the conversation and help generate solutions or changes)
>
> *we could implement* (you are in this together as their manager or supervisor)
>
> *take us* (again, it is a conversation involving you both)

Even the suggested response to raising their topic uses "we language:"

if we have time to discuss that now, we will

if not, we will schedule time for a separation conversation

It is essential to express that you and the team member are in this together. You both have a stake in wanting future success for the team member. And, even if the team member will do all of the implementation work and changes, it remains your responsibility to measure and monitor progress, provide additional coaching and feedback as necessary, recognize their efforts to improve, and reward improvements made.

Another area for planning how to manage the meeting includes determining how you will intentionally respond or act if the conversation becomes difficult, threatening, or dangerous. I will give you some best practices for this in the next chapter.

Planning the Progress Monitoring

Why is it important to establish the progress monitoring process at the end of each feedback conversation? Three reasons:

- It shows that you, as their manager, are committed to this process.

- It conveys to the team member that this area of their personal development is important enough to warrant ongoing monitoring.

- It provides an agreed-upon schedule as to when the ongoing monitoring and follow-up conversations will take place.

That last point is critical. Too often, the follow-up discussions are done ad hoc, usually when the manager has a free moment or suddenly realizes that they have not followed up or checked in with the team member recently.

When you reach out to the team member with an ad hoc and unexpected follow-up, you catch them unaware and unprepared for the discussion. It may not seem like a big deal to pick up the phone and ask, *"How is it going?" or "What progress have you made?"* type questions. And in reality, it may not be a big deal. However, it is usually highly ineffective!

Here is why. You will unlikely receive more than an "okay" or "fine" response. Or the person will give you shallow, top-of-the-mind answers regarding the progress they feel is being made. Or, even worse, they will respond with something they think you want to hear or that will appease you.

Additionally, since they did not anticipate this conversation, the team member might feel you are now micromanaging them. Or you feel they have slipped back or are not making the desired progress. After all, what prompted your sudden interest in having this conversation? From their perspective, the purpose or reason for you contacting them will likely be considered something negative.

Lastly, since you are likely to receive insubstantial and superficial replies, the conversation is not fruitful for either you or the team member. So yes, you did a check-in with your team member. But an ineffective and useless one. And perhaps even a relationship-damaging one if the team member feels your confidence in them has waned or they believe you have started micromanaging them.

As mentioned in the previous chapter, it is best to have regular progress monitoring reviews scheduled in advance. These should be based on specified time periods (e.g., every other Thursday) or specific milestones or deadlines (e.g., the initial presentation draft ready by a given date).

When these review discussions are planned and placed on your respective calendars, the team member is unlikely to feel they are being micromanaged. And you will feel more in control of their development process. You will also be prompted to plan the follow-up and progress monitoring discussions as you will know when these are scheduled.

Conversation Follow-Up

Another reason many feedback conversations are ineffective is that they end without a clear summary of actions and progress monitoring. In ineffective feedback conversations, the only actions identified are the ones to be taken by the team member. Remember, people development is a joint project and one of your most important responsibilities as a manager and leader.

Wrapping up and closing the conversation is a time for specifics. You want to ensure full clarity and agreement on the actions to be taken by each of you. You also want to establish an agreed timeline for how and when progress monitoring will happen.

Again, preparation and planning are key. How will you wrap up and summarize the discussion? Specific areas you want to ensure are covered in the wrap-up and summary close are:

- Reconfirmation of the specific actions to be taken by the team member.

- Restatement of the specific actions that you will take as their manager.

- Identifying how progress monitoring will take place and the timing of such.

- Expressions of gratitude from you and that you are confident that the actions you both will take will lead to desired results.

- Thanking them for their participation in the discussion and for the ideas, suggestions, and insights they have provided.

Another key to success is to summarize and document these specific actions and the monitoring process in writing within 24 hours of the discussion. This written confirmation is not for cover-your-backside purposes. It is done to provide both you and the team member with a clear, written confirmation of what has been agreed. The goal is to ensure a clear understanding (and prevent any possible misunderstanding) of the actions and progress monitoring.

When sending the written confirmation to the team member, keep your tone neutral, use "we language," and give the team member 48 hours to reply with any questions or differences in interpretation of what was agreed. Here is my simple formula for this written confirmation:

Thank you again (name) for our productive conversation yesterday on (topic).

As we agreed, you will:

- *Action one (with a deadline if agreed)*
- *Action two (with a deadline if agreed)*
- *Action three (with a deadline if agreed)*

And I will:

- *Action one (with a deadline if agreed)*
- *Action two (with a deadline if agreed)*
- *Action three (with a deadline if agreed)*

Additionally, we will meet again to review progress and future steps:

- *When XX has been accomplished*

(or)

- *On (date/time)*

(or)

- *Every (date/time) or every other (date/time)*

Please revert to me by (date) if you have any questions, anything to add, or any different takeaways from our discussion.

Again, I believe these actions will achieve the results we both desire.

Best regards,
Name

By keeping the written confirmation simple and using neutral language, this message delivers the simple purpose of reconfirming the key actions and progress monitoring process. And it does so without appearing to be a "record for the file" or a "cover my backside" communication.

Planning the Progress Monitoring Conversations

Preparing and planning for the follow-up discussions is straightforward. The items you want to discuss include the following:

- What progress have they made on the actions agreed upon?

- What hurdles or obstacles are they facing regarding these actions?

- What help or assistance do they need from you to either continue making progress or to overcome identifiable hurdles and obstacles?

- What progress have you made on the actions agreed, and did this have the intended consequences for the team member?

- Is the team member aware of the progress you have made on your agreed actions?

- What ideas or suggestions does the team member have for any changes in their actions?

- What ideas or suggestions does the team member have for any additional support or assistance they need from you?

- Discussion and agreement on the next steps.

- Confirmation on the next progress monitoring conversation.

A great question to always include in the conversation is, *"What are the three things I could do (as your leader) to help you make substantial progress in the coming weeks?"*

This is an example of a High Impact Question. High Impact Questions are designed to entice the other person to evaluate, analyze, speculate, and think deeply. You do not get off-the-top-of-the-head, reactive responses to High Impact Questions.

Rather, the responses to High Impact Questions provide depth of information and insights that cannot be gained or gleaned elsewhere.

As you can see, this is more than a *"How is it going?"* conversation. This is why you must prepare in advance what you want to say, what questions you want to include, what follow-up questions you want to ask, and any suggestions you have for future actions and progress monitoring.

Everything mentioned previously regarding rapport building, wrapping up, summarizing the conversation, and expressing gratitude, thanks, and confidence applies in these follow-up conversations.

77

:

Preparing the Environment

Naturally, you will want to ensure a private and psychologically safe environment for all feedback discussions, particularly Enhancement Feedback ones.

There are other aspects of the environment that many people do not consider.

For instance, avoiding a large physical barrier between you and your team member is best. This includes shunning large round tables, a conference room table, or even your office desk in face-to-face conversations. Hence, a neutral room with a small table is preferable. Or, if you are having the discussion in your office, consider stepping out from behind your desk and sitting closer to one another.

When possible, select a room with no windows. Or one with curtains or blinds. You want to minimize being distracted by people walking by the room. Also, the team member will feel more comfortable knowing that others cannot look into the room or observe the conversation.

Turn your instant messaging system setting to unavailable or other settings for virtual feedback conversations. And turn off your email notifications and anything else that might distract you from being fully present in the conversation.

Likewise, for all feedback discussions, put your mobile devices on silent mode (or, better yet, on airplane mode).

If you think this will be a conversation in which emotions or tears might arise, be sure to have a tissue box in the room. I advise placing the tissue box midway between you and the team member. It should be off to one side, not directly in the middle between the two of you. Having bottled water in the room is another best practice.

You want to create an environment that feels safe, comfortable, and as neutral as possible. It should also minimize or prevent distractions, thus enabling you both to be fully present throughout the conversation. You also want the environment to enhance connectedness and encourage an open, transparent, and robust dialogue.

The final environment you need to prepare is your mindset.

Preparing Your Mindset

How you approach each feedback conversation will greatly impact its effectiveness and eventual outcomes. This is why getting your mindset completely set is so critical.

First of all, your mindset as you prepare and then enter the feedback conversation should be that your purpose is straightforward: you want to help the other person discover and determine ways to improve their capabilities, competencies, and confidence. If you have any other purpose in mind, you should reconsider having the conversation.

So, if you intend to give (not share) feedback to show who the boss is, or to belittle someone, you should definitely forego the talk. The same applies if your purpose of giving feedback is to blame and shame someone or merely to point out the mistakes they have made.

Additionally, part of setting your mindset is to ensure your emotions are under control. As a human being, you have the right to your emotions. Thus, you have the right to be angry, disappointed, upset, irate, furious, or any other emotion when someone has performed poorly and acted inappropriately. However, unleashing these emotions while sharing feedback can result in defensiveness or retaliatory emotions from the other person.

Managing the expression of our emotions reveals our emotional intelligence levels. As I wrote in *Humony Leadership: Mindsets, Skills, and Behaviors for Being a Successful People-Centric Leader*, emotional intelligence is not a soft skill. It is a hard-edged leadership skill that provides high-value and bottom-line results. It is the true affect and impact we have on those around us, a critical skill that brings out our best performance and allows us to bring out the best in those we lead.

Research indicates that effective leaders have a high degree of emotional intelligence. I believe emotional intelligence is a cornerstone skill for leaders, particularly when engaging in feedback conversations.

Another important aspect of your mindset as you enter a feedback discussion is acceptance. You must accept the other person's right to decide whether to make a change or which changes to make. Everyone has the right to accept, partially accept, or decline feedback.

Everyone also has the right not to change, except for mandatory areas, as stipulated earlier:

- Ethical matters
- Legal matters and violations
- Safety issues
- Compliance policies
- Socially inappropriate behavior or comments
- Processes that must be followed
- Anything with major financial or reputational risk implications

Of course, our role as managers and leaders is to ensure that our team members fully understand the potential negative consequences of not changing their actions, attitudes, or behaviors. As adults, they are responsible for the consequences and repercussions of their actions or nonactions.

Always remember, if your team member decides not to make a change, this is not a rejection of you or your leadership skills. While this is frequently disappointing when it happens, you should never take this personally. You should, however, review the discussions held with this person to analyze and evaluate how the conversations might have gone differently.

You also want to review these discussions to ensure you did not skip any of the steps in the Effective Feedback Model and that you appropriately documented the action items and progress monitoring process in writing. Lastly, if you have followed these processes and shared feedback on an ongoing, continuous basis with this recalcitrant team member, then you can rest assured you have done your best.

Preparing Your Mental Presence

As you enter any feedback conversation, it is imperative your mental focus is 100% present in the discussion.

That means you have to set aside all other thoughts, including those emails that need responding and those important requests from your boss.

You can begin preparing your mental presence while going through the environment preparation steps above. Take deep, purposeful breaths as you shut down electronic and other distractions. Sometimes referred to as Rhythmic Breathing or concentrated breathing, Purposeful Breathing helps reduce multiple thoughts and enables us to concentrate on a single thought or task.

Whether you call it purposeful breathing, rhythmic breathing, abdominal breathing, diaphragmatic breathing, or simply deep breathing, a conscious breathing pattern of deep breaths increases the oxygen supply to the brain. It also stimulates the parasympathetic nervous system, which promotes a state of calmness.

Breathing more deeply and at a slower pace has been proven to have several benefits, including relaxing tension in the body, calming nervous shaking, and decreasing blood pressure. Purposeful Breathing also helps you feel connected to your body while simultaneously washing away the worries in your head and quieting your mind. As a result, it can help you feel more confident as you enter the feedback discussion.

You want to enter the feedback conversation fully present and remain that way – as much as possible – throughout the entire conversation. Do not worry if your mind starts to wander now and then. That is natural. Fortunately, it is also easy to bring the mind back to full attention with deliberate and concerted effort.

When the other person notices your full presence in the conversation, they will be appreciative. Being fully present also signals to the other person the importance of the conversation and that this is not a check-box activity that neither of you wants to rush through.

Managing the Conversation

Undoubtedly, some feedback conversations can become difficult, even argumentative or threatening. That is why you want to prepare in advance how you will manage the conversation if emotions run high or the discussion goes off course.

As discussed above in *Planning the Conversation*, there are three components of the discussion you need to manage:

- Building rapport at the start
- The flow of the discussion

:

- Wrapping up and summarizing the next steps at the close

Knowing in advance how you want to manage these three parts creates more fruitful and productive discussions. Hence, it is important to plan each of these three critical components. Planning and preparing cannot be over-emphasized.

Frankly, proper planning and preparation are the only ways to ensure you manage the conversation toward an effective outcome, despite whatever ebbs and flows crop up. This also helps ensure you do not wander into unchartered territory on issues, problems, or complaints you are unprepared to handle.

Remember, this is a feedback conversation, not a feedback meeting. Nothing dictates the entire feedback conversation must occur in a single discussion. In fact, it is often best to have several discussions over several days or a week. Another decisive component of managing effective feedback conversations is knowing when to break off the discussion and adjourn to another day and time.

For instance, what usually happens when a manager receives no reply or shrugged shoulders in response to the question, *"What suggestions do you have for how we can make improvements in this area?"* Typically, the manager will see this as an opening to proffer their own solutions and directions. Please avoid this temptation.

The best practice for managers, supervisors, and leaders would be something along the lines of the following:

You know, this is important for both of us. Let's both think of some potential solutions and give this more thought. How about we regroup in two days? How does Thursday at 10am work for you? Great, I look forward to hearing your thoughts and ideas then.

Note the "we" language here. Also note the positive, upbeat finish. Most importantly, note the emphasis on hearing from the other person, reinforcing your commitment to listen to them and their ideas. This builds trust and enhances the relationship between you and the other person. It connotates that you and the other person are in this important improvement process together. Performance improvement is a team sport, with you both as co-partners in the process.

Correctly ending the discussion this way paves the way for a highly productive subsequent session. Should the other person not have any suggestions or ideas to share at this next session, put yours on the table for discussion. The key word here is "discussion." You want to offer your ideas as possible solutions, not mandated actions.

Whichever way the conversation goes, always be sure to end it on a positive note. Also, be sure to bring it to a complete close, focusing only on the feedback discussion. Do not bring up other topics, check on work status, or ask if there is anything else they want to discuss. Those are subjects for another discussion, no matter how tempting it is to raise them since you are already engaged in a conversation.

Put aside such temptations. This was an important conversation on an important topic. Do not dilute its importance and significance by discussing other topics. You want them to think – even if subconsciously – about the situation and impact discussed and how to move forward with positive progress. Do not let other topics or issues interfere with their conscious and subconscious thoughts.

Additionally, be sure to thank them for their involvement in the discussion. Be specific in referencing any ideas, data, explanations, or thoughts they shared. Then, end the meeting promptly with courtesy and a smile of appreciation!

The Importance of Practice

The other successful factor for having effective communication is practice. Unfortunately, too many conversations in the workplace happen on an ad hoc or spur-of-the-moment basis.

Like preparation, practice is often an overlooked element. It should not be.

You want to practice:

- The questions you want to raise
- Follow-up questions, particularly when you can anticipate the response to a question but need to dig deeper for other root causes or extenuating circumstances
- The phraseology of the key points you want to make
- How you will balance advocacy (expressing your viewpoint and perspective) and inquiry

(seeking the other person's viewpoint and perspective)

- How you will communicate the examples and specific incidents you want to share without denoting blame or implying shame

- Your body language to demonstrate that you are fully present and listening to the other person

- The tonality of your voice to express that this is an important and serious conversation, and one that is neither minor nor devastating

- Responses to questions or accusations you expect to be raised by the other person

- Biting your tongue to prevent you from saying the things you do not want to say

- How you will maintain composure, calmness, and steadiness if emotions or argumentativeness arises

- How you will segue from the opening rapport stage to the specifics of the feedback discussion

- How you will raise the specifics of the progress monitoring and suggest when the progress monitoring discussions will take place

- How you will close off the discussion, either through adjourning to another day and time or by wrapping up and summarizing

You will also want to practice how you will handle things if the conversation goes astray or becomes difficult. That is the subject of the next chapter.

CHAPTER 5

Handling Difficult Conversations

Unfortunately, no matter how much you prepare or plan, not every feedback conversation will go smoothly. After all, human personalities, quirks, emotions, attitudes, and differing perspectives are all brought to bear in every feedback conversation.

Difficult feedback situations happen when any of the following arise:

- Anger
- Crying
- Extreme disagreement
- Blaming of others
- Refusal to accept responsibility for actions, behaviors, or results
- Physical threats
- Verbal abuse
- Snarky comments
- Negative body language

- The other person cannot, or will not, think of possible solutions or offer ideas

- Disengagement

- Disinterest

Preparing in advance to handle these and other troubling situations is crucial for success. Even the most problematic and challenging conversations can be managed with proper planning, a strong mindset, and knowing in advance how you will manage sticky situations.

Always remember that effective feedback is a process, not a one-time discussion. You do not need to reach a resolution or an agreement on actions in one conversation. Knowing this reduces the pressure to reach a conclusion or solution in the first feedback discussion. It also provides you the confidence to adjourn the discussion whenever emotions hit a boiling point, or you feel uncomfortable about your physical or emotional safety.

Here are some best practices to help you formulate strategies and tactics to prepare for conversations that might take an unfortunate wrong turn.

The Importance of Self-Confidence

Dealing with an emotional outburst from the other person is a common fear about feedback conversations. This fear often leads managers, supervisors, and leaders to delay giving 'negative' feedback. However, with self-confidence, you can approach these situations with a strong mindset and the intention to help the other person improve.

As mentioned earlier, the key to overcoming the fear of giving 'negative' feedback is to eliminate the use of the terms positive and negative from your feedback vocabulary. Remember, your feedback is intended to assist the other person in their improvement journey. There is no negativity in this intention.

Having a mindset that you will give (not share) negative (instead of enhancement) feedback automatically lowers your self-confidence. After all, it is doubtful that you wake up in the morning thinking, "I cannot wait to give so-and-so negative feedback today." Reluctance to have a feedback conversation leads to diminished self-assurance. And this hesitancy will be noticed by the other person, prompting them to jump on any perceived weaknesses in your fortitude and belief in what you want to express in the conversation.

Approaching the feedback conversation with tentativeness and timidity helps create the difficult conversations that managers, supervisors, and leaders are so afraid of. Hence, in many ways, such insecure and self-doubting leaders contribute significantly to feedback conversations going askew and off course.

So, while you cannot prevent feedback discussions from becoming tough and difficult, you can minimize the impact through your self-confidence, poise, composure, and prepared self-control.

Best Practices for Handling Difficult Conversations

When emotions arise during a feedback conversation, do not fuel the fire by pointing this out through your words or actions. Remember, everyone has a right to their emotions and feelings. On the other hand, everyone must take responsibility and accountability for how they choose to express their emotions and feelings.

While it may seem empathetic to offer a consoling statement along the lines of *"I can see this is upsetting you,"* refrain from such statements. Doing so will only lead to another argument as they instinctively claim, *"No, it is not."* As a result, instead of talking about the nucleus of the feedback subject, you will fall into a tangential discussion about whether the other person is upset or emotionally distraught.

Additionally, do not offer tissues to the other person. Let them reach for one on their own. This is why I recommend putting the tissue box off to one side, near the middle of the table, within easy reach of both participants.

There will be times when you want to enable the other person to regain control of their emotions and thoughts. My trick for handling this is to say, *"I need to refresh my coffee. Do you mind if I step out for 2-3 minutes and get more coffee? Would you like me to get you anything as well?"*

With this technique, I can show empathy without pointing out their emotional state. This pause usually takes 4-6 minutes, sufficient time for most people to recapture a sense of calmness and recover emotional equanimity.

When emotions start getting out of hand, or the other person refuses to engage in the conversation, it is much better to abruptly end the conversation with a statement along the lines of:

> *This is important for both of us. Let's both of us give this some more thought and regroup in two days. How does Wednesday at 4pm work for you?*

> *Great, I look forward to hearing and discussing your thoughts and ideas. And I also welcome your ideas and suggestions for possible solutions and improvements we can implement.*

As in the example in the previous chapter, note the use of "we" language. Also, note the emphasis on listening and discussing the other person's thoughts and ideas. Lastly, this structure invites the other person to share ideas and suggestions for improvement in the next conversation, even if you have not reached that step in the Effective Feedback Model. You are prompting them to think of potential solutions that can be implemented jointly. Most importantly, you give them a heads-up that you want to hear their ideas and suggestions.

Sometimes, moving in this direction will prompt their immediate cooperation and collaboration. They may even respond, *"No, let's continue now. I'm okay."* In such instances, this is your judgment call to make. You are their leader, and you are in control of the conversation. Whether to continue

:

now or postpone until later is your call and your call only. Be resolute in your decision. And express it nonjudgmentally yet assertively.

If you decide to defer to another session, I recommend agreeing on a time that is 36-40 hours in the future. This provides two nights of sleep to allow your respective unconscious thoughts to percolate and any emotional tensions to wane. Continuing the conversation the next day is usually too soon and should be avoided.

However, suppose you are working in geographically separate locations and it is impossible to meet face-to-face again in two days. In that case, a meeting the next day should be considered a viable option.

More than two days is usually too long to keep the conversation fresh and the momentum moving in the right direction. The exception to this will be when the initial conversation takes place on a Friday or the day before a holiday weekend. In such cases, the following Monday or the next working day is your best option for the subsequent conversation.

Whatever the circumstances and your decision, be sure to lock in the day and time of the next conversation. Do not let this be something that is confirmed at a later time. These are important conversations – and this is an important process – which is more clearly communicated when you confirm the timing of the ensuing conversation.

Never Put Personal Safety At Risk

Rarely – and hopefully never – you may feel that a feedback conversation has put your personal safety at risk.

Never, never, never allow such a situation to escalate or intensify. At the first sign of feeling threatened or in danger, immediately rise, state your unease, abruptly end the meeting, and walk away without looking back or responding to any comments.

As you do so, use neutral and non-threatening words such as:

> *I am feeling uncomfortable with the tonality and direction of this conversation.*
>
> *I think it is best to stop here and meet again in a couple of days. I will reach out with a day and time to continue.*
>
> *Thank you for your time today.*

Note the total lack of "we" language. This is a time for you to be assertive and direct. However, no accusations (I am feeling threatened by you). And no pointing of blame. You are taking responsibility and accountability. You are in charge. Make your point and head straight for the door.

Do not look back or respond in any way if the other person starts shouting, calling you names (coward, weakling), taunting you, or throwing out apologies for their words or behavior. What has happened has happened. Walk away and

:

maintain as much poise, calm, and self-control as you can muster. The time for interaction is over, at least for now.

Your responsibility at this point is to look after your own mental, emotional, physical, and spiritual wellbeing. Undoubtedly, you will feel increased stress and a range of other emotions. What is your go-to method for calming yourself down? Use whatever works for you, such as:

- going outside for some fresh air and sunshine
- 5-10 minutes of Purposeful Breathing
- talking with a friend or colleague
- meditation
- taking a walk
- listening to soft music
- hitting the gym
- writing your thoughts and feelings down on paper

Your priority at this moment is you. Do not rush into another meeting or call. Clear your calendar for the next hour or two if needed. As you start to calm down, congratulate yourself for responding to the situation and the individual instead of reacting. Then, when you are ready, rehash the discussion in your mind and analyze what went wrong and why. Do not look for blame. Just the root causes.

And consider what you might say or do differently in such a situation in the future. This is a time for reflection, not action. Hold off the impulse to reach out to the other person or anyone else in the organization, including Human Resources (unless you feel physically threatened, violated, or in danger, in which case proceed to HR or contact your Security Department immediately).

When it comes to the subsequent meeting, you have two choices. You can meet again in a one-to-one conversation or bring in a third person as a mediator or protector. Either way is your choice.

However you decide to proceed, you do not need to apologize for terminating the previous meeting and walking away. Nor should you demand an apology from the other person. If they wish to apologize for their actions or words, allow that to happen. Accept their apology with gratitude and a simple "thank you." Then, start the meeting with your agenda (probably continuing where you left off) and the desired outcome you have for this conversation.

If you think it appropriate, you might establish ground rules for appropriate behavior, language, demeanor, and body language. Again, this is your choice.

Such ground rules should also include the actions you will take (such as walking away again or taking a break) should they be violated. This is a good method for establishing expectations and the consequences of inappropriate behavior or words.

Do not feel you are being cowardly should you bring a third person into the conversation as an observer, facilitator, mediator, witness, or protector. Only foolish people try to exhibit courage by putting themselves purposely in a dangerous situation. Your intention is to help the other person improve, not show how tough or fearless you are.

As you re-enter the conversation, remember that the goal is to create a dialogue, not deliver a monologue. This is why the mindset that you will be "sharing feedback" and not "giving feedback" is so important, even when anticipating difficult and challenging discussions.

Plus, as in everything you do in communicating as a leader, preparation and practice are essential to your success. Hence, prepare thoroughly for how you want to restart the conversation, the ground rules you will establish, and your plan of action if the conversation deteriorates again to the point you feel unsafe.

And, while engaged in the conversation, the two indispensable communication skills to utilize are asking questions (including follow-up questions) and listening. These skills produce effective dialogues and help the other person decide what and how to implement changes that lead to greater results for them, your team, and the organization.

CHAPTER 6

It's Up To You

Feedback is one of the most powerful levers available to managers and leaders for growing and developing people. However, to reap its benefits, you must use this tool effectively.

Here is some research that might surprise you:

> A 10-year, groundbreaking study of 200,000 managers and employees by the O.C. Tanner Group revealed that 79% of employees who quit their jobs cited a lack of appreciation as a key reason.

> That same study also disclosed that 65% of North Americans reported that they were not recognized *even once* by their leaders or supervisors over the previous year.

This is inexcusable and unacceptable.

One of your responsibilities as a people leader is to catch people doing things well. Always recognize the efforts of your team members through Fortifying Feedback. Doing so prompts self-satisfaction and self-confidence in them, combining the powers of extrinsic (your recognition of their efforts) and intrinsic (their satisfaction and confidence) motivation to propel future good work.

The three Ps of preparation, planning, and practice are the keys to having outstanding feedback conversations that lead to action and change. Ensuring you take the time to prepare, plan, and practice for your feedback conversations turns feedback into a gift that keeps on giving for both you and your team member.

Here are the Golden Rules for effective feedback:

1. Invest your time preparing, planning, and practicing for your feedback conversations.

2. Share feedback often and regularly (my rule is that everyone should receive Fortifying or Enhancement feedback at least once every three weeks).

3. As much as practical, keep Fortifying and Enhancement Feedback discussions as separate conversations. Drop the so-called sandwich approach to feedback.

4. Approach feedback conversations with the intention of helping someone determine how to improve their performance, behavior, or results.

5. Enter all feedback conversations with a fully present and positive mindset.

6. Ensure the critical elements of importance and impact are covered in all feedback conversations.

7. Feedback conversations are to be dialogues resulting in optimal exchange of information, perspectives, ideas, and possible actions.

8. Feedback is a team sport. Use "we" language.

9. Document all your Enhancement Feedback conversations in writing, highlighting the actions and timelines agreed upon and the timing of the progress monitoring conversations.

There is no excuse for giving ineffective feedback. It takes only four – albeit four critical – elements to provide effective feedback:

1. Mindset changes

2. A new language and terminology around feedback

3. An effective and proven feedback model and process

4. Proper planning, preparation, and practice

These four critical elements and dozens of other tips, techniques, and best practices have been shared with you in *The Art of Effective Feedback*. Now, it is up to you to utilize these to the best of your ability. And remember, like any skill, you will get better at effective feedback through practice, implementation, reflection, and more practice.

Then, you will realize the numerous benefits of Effective Feedback, including:

- Individual and team development

- Elimination of hurdles and obstacles preventing goal attainment

- Stronger relationships between managers and team members

- Higher employee morale

:

- Increased collaboration, innovation, creativity, and results

- Increased employee retention and, thus, a reduction in expenses related to replacing employees who quit

Remember, effective feedback requires time, commitment, and courage. Fortunately, the reward is the continuous growth of your people and the creation of a thriving development and performance culture for your team and organization.

You will become a better leader by changing your mindset, language, and methodology for sharing feedback with your direct reports, colleagues, and others. The results will be increased employee engagement, innovation, creativity, collaboration, loyalty, and achieving your goals and objectives.

Go forth and become the Great Leader you know you can be.

Steven Howard Quotes
on Leadership

Never stop learning because life never stops teaching.

Great leaders are not afraid of mistakes or failures. They are only afraid of not learning from mistakes and failures.

Peace of mind in the workplace is not the absence of conflict but the ability to cope with it without drama or victimization.

Leadership is not a position, title, or spot on an organizational chart. Leadership is a skill to be developed, practiced, and enhanced.

It is not what happens that defines you; it is what you do next.

Don't be a prisoner of your past. Be the architect of your future.

You are your life's most important variable.

You are the only one holding you back.

Progress is less about speed and much more about direction.

When feedback is combined with forgiveness, leaders are more likely to prompt and motivate changes that result in better performance and improved behavior.

One of the greatest gifts a leader can give to team members is to help them find and grow their talents.

Continuous training of your employees, especially in the "soft skills" areas of teamwork, collaboration, and working across boundaries, is the key to scaling every part of your business.

Leaders who don't listen will eventually be surrounded by people unwilling to speak and contribute.

The true measure of team leadership is not about how many team members are working but how well they are working together.

A team is not a group of people who work together. A team is a group of people working together towards a shared outcome who trust and respect each other.

Your greatness does not need to be proven. Only exhibited.

Mistakes are an iterative part of life. Mistakes will not define who you are. Responding and recovering from mistakes do.

Wisdom is not about knowing all the answers. Wisdom is asking the right questions of the right person or people.

No one is unflawed or perfect. Flaws are charming and likable. Accept your flaws. Admit your mistakes. Doing so will not hurt you. But their denial and cover-up will.

As you move into higher leadership positions, your network is part of your net worth to your organization and your team.

Don't base your desired outcome only on income. Do some good.

Acknowledgments

I want to recognize and thank the leaders with whom I have worked whose thoughts and behaviors have influenced my thinking on leadership: April Arnzen (Micron Technology), Deirdre Ball (Reader's Digest and The Financial Times), Al Bond (Texas Instruments), Nancy Elder (formerly MasterCard, now NY Mets), Goh Geok Ling (Texas Instruments), Jonathon Gould (MasterCard), Steinar Hjelle (formerly Micron Technology, now Boise Cascade), Ron Mahoney (Texas Instruments), William Malloy (Forum Corporation), Rodrigo S. Martineli (formerly Hewlett-Packard Enterprise and Rackspace Technology, now Stefanini Group), Shisho Matsushima (TIME Magazine), David McAuliffe (TIME Magazine), Ed Morrett (Texas Instruments), Ralph Oliva (Texas Instruments), André Sekulic (MasterCard), David Smith (Citibank), Rana Talwar (Citibank), Georgette Tan (MasterCard), Todd Taylor (formerly HPE, now the University of Notre Dame), and Frank Walters (Texas Instruments).

About the Author

Steven Howard is an award-winning author of 25 leadership, business, marketing, and professional development books. In awarding his book *Humony Leadership: Mindsets, Skills, and Behaviors for Being a Success People-Centric Leader* a Gold Medal, the Nonfiction Authors Association called it "a significant work with an important mission."

Humony is a word created by Steven comprising Human, Humanity, and Harmony to emphasize the leading of people and the need for leaders to create workplaces of wellbeing and harmony.

His book *Better Decisions Better Thinking Better Outcomes: How to go from Mind Full to Mindful Leadership*, received a Silver Award from the Nonfiction Authors Association. He also wrote *Leadership Lessons from the Volkswagen Saga*, which won three prestigious publishing industry awards (2017 Independent Press Award, National Indie Excellence Award, and San Francisco Book Festival Award).

Steven is also the author of *Great Leadership Words of Wisdom* and co-author of *Strong Women Speak on Leadership, Success and Living Well: Lessons for Life from Strong Women Through the Ages*.

Steven was named one of the 2023 Top 200 Global Biggest Voices in Leadership in recognition of his thought-provoking and leading-edge thinking on leadership. He was also named to the 2023 CREA List of Top Influential Leaders for his thought leadership and writing.

His corporate career covered a wide variety of fields and experiences, including Regional Marketing Director for Texas Instruments Asia-Pacific, Regional Director South Asia for TIME Magazine, Global Account Director at BBDO Advertising handling an international airline account, and VP Marketing for Citibank's Consumer Banking Group.

In the past 25 years, he has mentored, coached, and trained over 12,500 leaders in Asia, Australia, Africa, Europe, Mexico, and North America.

He brings a truly international, cross-cultural perspective to his clients, having lived in the USA for over 30 years, in Singapore for 21 years, in Australia for 12 years, and in Mexico City (3 years).

Contact Details

Email: steven@CalienteLeadership.com

Twitter: @stevenbhoward | @GreatLeadershp

LinkedIn: www.linkedin.com/in/stevenbhoward

YouTube:

https://www.youtube.com/@stevenhowardonleadership

Website: www.CalienteLeadership.com

Website: www.HumonyLeadership.com

Instagram: @HumonyLeadership